JODI MILLIGAN

Keys to Buying Your First Home

*Practical Step-by-Step Tips from a Licensed Realtor®
and Mortgage Loan Originator*

Copyright © 2024 by Jodi Milligan

All rights reserved. No part of this publication may be reproduced, stored or transmitted in any form or by any means, electronic, mechanical, photocopying, recording, scanning, or otherwise without written permission from the publisher. It is illegal to copy this book, post it to a website, or distribute it by any other means without permission.

Jodi Milligan asserts the moral right to be identified as the author of this work.

Jodi Milligan has no responsibility for the persistence or accuracy of URLs for external or third-party Internet Websites referred to in this publication and does not guarantee that any content on such Websites is, or will remain, accurate or appropriate.

Designations used by companies to distinguish their products are often claimed as trademarks. All brand names and product names used in this book and on its cover are trade names, service marks, trademarks and registered trademarks of their respective owners. The publishers and the book are not associated with any product or vendor mentioned in this book. None of the companies referenced within the book have endorsed the book.

First edition

This book was professionally typeset on Reedsy.
Find out more at reedsy.com

Contents

1	Introduction	1
2	Preparation Phase–Determining Affordability	3
3	House Hunting Phase: Finding a Home	8
4	Due-Diligence Phase	13
5	Securing Financing Phase	17
6	Closing Phase	24
7	Conclusion and Re-Cap	27
8	Glossary	29
	About the Author	32

1

Introduction

Are you ready to purchase a new home? Really ready? If you are a first time home buyer, the information in this book will guide you through the entire process and will help you avoid making mistakes that could potentially cause the whole thing to fall through.

My name is Jodi Milligan, I have been a licensed Realtor® in Memphis, TN since 2006 and a licensed Mortgage Loan Originator since 2021. My favorite clients are those who are first time home buyers. I love educating them on the various aspects of the home buying and mortgage process making sure they understand the terms and the steps needed in this wonderful quest of becoming a homeowner.

This book contains detailed steps and key information that will make the process go super smoothly. When you see this 🔑, take special note. This indicates an important thing to remember. If a word is written in italics, it is defined in the glossary section at the end of the book.

The less prepared you are, the more stressful buying a home will be.

Let's get prepared!

2

Preparation Phase–Determining Affordability

Searching for a home is a really fun aspect of buying a home. I always enjoy looking at homes for sale no matter if it's for a client or just for fun. However, it is not the first step in purchasing a home.

🗝 **Before you begin seriously looking for a home, you must know what you can afford.**

One of the most important factors in determining if you will be able to obtain financing for a home purchase is your *credit score*. Credit scores are used by lenders to assess an individual's creditworthiness and financial reliability. They range from 300 to 850 with a higher score being the best. Your credit score will affect the type of loan you can qualify for as well as the interest rate of your loan. Your lender will run a *credit report* that will tell them your credit score.

Another factor that is equally important is your *debt-to-income ratio (DTI)*. The DTI expressed as a percentage. It is calculated by dividing your monthly debt (mortgage or potential mortgage, homeowner's insurance, property taxes, credit card minimum monthly payments, car notes, student loan monthly payments, etc) by your monthly *gross income*. Gross income is the total amount of money earned by an individual before any deductions or taxes are taken out. This is used to determine your ability to manage monthly payments and repay debts. The lower the percentage the better.

Example:
Monthly Debt
Mortgage $1500
Home Owner's Insurance $150
Property Taxes $200
Credit Card Min $200
Car note $400
Total Monthly Debt $2450
Gross Monthly Income $6500
$2450/$6500=37.69
DTI is 37.69%

🔑 **If your credit score is under 580 or your DTI is greater than 43%, consider paying off some of your debt and/or contacting a credit agency who can give you tips on how to raise your credit score.**

How do I know what price I can afford?

The next and most important step is to get pre-approved for a loan. This will determine what price house you can afford.

How do I get pre-approved for a loan?

PREPARATION PHASE–DETERMINING AFFORDABILITY

To get pre-approved for a loan, you will need to find a lender. There are a couple of ways to look for a lender. You can use a Mortgage Loan Originator, a bank, or a national lender. It is important to find one who will give you the best service. The worst thing that can happen is for your loan to fall through.

A **Mortgage Loan Originator (MLO)** is a licensed broker who can look for a variety of loans and determine which type loan you can qualify for based on your credit score and debt to income ratio. A MLO has access to many different lenders and can shop around to find a loan that best meets your financial needs. The best way to find a mortgage broker is to ask for recommendations from those you trust and to read reviews. You can also visit **www.mortgagematchup.com** to find a broker in your area.

Another option is to use a **local bank** with which you have a relationship. They are local, which is helpful. However, banks typically do not have the ability to shop around to get the best interest rate and product for your individual needs.

A **national lender** (Rocket Mortgage, Quicken, ext) is a large company who services all over. They claim to have the best interest rates, but are not always up front about their fees.

It's best to have a local lender who can give you the personal service you deserve and who will be available to answer any questions you may have. Another advantage to having a local lender is that if an issue arises at the last minute, they are able to handle it in a more timely manner.

🔑**Use a local lender or Mortgage Loan Originator.**

What will the lender need from me?

The lender will need several things from you in order to give you a pre-approval letter.

- **Permission to pull your credit report.** This will give a detailed account of credit history along with a numerical score (300-850, the higher the score, the better). If your score is under 600, you need to work on bringing it up before purchasing a home
- **Proof of income:** Pay stubs, W-2 forms, and tax returns for the past two years.
- **Proof of assets:** Bank statements and investment account statements to verify savings and other assets.
- **Employment verification:** Recent pay stubs or a letter from your employer.
- **Debt information:** Information about existing debts, such as credit card balances, car loans, and student loans. You will be required to give statements of open accounts.
- **Identification:** A government-issued ID, such as a driver's license or passport.

How do I make sure the process goes smoothly?

- **Maintain Financial Stability:** Avoid making large purchases or opening new credit accounts during the pre-approval process until you close on the house.
- **Be Honest and Accurate:** Provide accurate information on your application to avoid delays or denials.
- **Stay Organized:** Keep all your financial documents organized and readily available for the lender.

PREPARATION PHASE–DETERMINING AFFORDABILITY

Following these steps will help you get pre-approved for a mortgage, giving you a clear understanding of your budget and making you a more attractive buyer in the competitive housing market.

3

House Hunting Phase: Finding a Home

Should I hire a Real Estate Agent?

There are pros and cons to using a Real Estate Agent to help you purchase a home. For first time home buyers, it is definitely recommended to use an agent. Check with your local Board of Realtors® to see if the seller pays for the agent's commission. If so, definitely use an agent since you will not be paying the commission.

Pros:

- Real estate agents have extensive knowledge of the local market, including current trends, property values, and neighborhoods.
- They can provide insights and guidance throughout the home-buying process.
- Agents have access to multiple listing services (MLS), which offer a comprehensive database of available properties. Some areas have systems where an agent can set up a portal for you where new listings or price changes of houses that meet your specific criteria will automatically alert you.

HOUSE HUNTING PHASE: FINDING A HOME

- They can identify homes that meet your criteria and arrange viewings.
- Experienced agents are skilled negotiators who can help you get the best price and terms. They can handle negotiations on your behalf, which can be particularly beneficial in competitive markets.
- Real estate transactions involve a lot of paperwork, including contracts, disclosures, and inspection reports. Agents can help you navigate and understand these documents, ensuring everything is completed accurately.
- Agents often have a network of professionals, such as mortgage brokers, home inspectors, and attorneys, which can streamline the buying process. They can recommend trusted service providers.
- Agents can save you time by doing the legwork, such as researching properties, scheduling viewings, and coordinating with other parties involved in the transaction.

Cons:

- Real estate agents earn a commission, usually paid by the seller, but sometimes costs are factored into the overall price of the home.
- Some buyers prefer to have full control over their home search and negotiations.
- Working with an agent means relying on their schedule and approach, which may not always align with your preferences.
- The quality and experience of agents can vary significantly, so it's crucial to research and select a reputable agent with a proven track record.
- Some agents may pressure clients to make quick decisions or settle for properties that don't fully meet their needs.

Using a real estate agent can provide significant advantages, especially for first-time buyers or those unfamiliar with the local market. Selecting a knowledgeable, trustworthy agent who understands your needs and communicates effectively is key to a positive home-buying experience. Ask friends and family for recommendations.

How do I search for a home?

Using a licensed real estate agent is highly recommended. The agent might ask you to sign a buyer's representation agreement which will give them a clear understanding of your wants and needs. It also ensures that they will be compensated for their services. The following are things you need to communicate with the agent.

- Your must-haves (e.g., number of bedrooms, bathrooms, location) and nice-to-haves (e.g., a swimming pool, a large backyard).
- Prioritize: Rank your preferences to help narrow down your search.
- Location Matters: Consider factors like proximity to work, schools, public transportation, amenities, and overall safety.

The agent will begin searching for homes that meet your criteria. Showings of those homes can be scheduled by the agent. You will meet your agent at the property to view it.

What do I look for when looking at a home for the first time?

1. The location— Are the surrounding homes and yards well-kept? Is the street busy or near a busy street? Is it in a safe area of town?
2. The floor plan—Does the layout fit your needs? Does it have the number of bedrooms and bathrooms you need? Do you like the kitchen, bathrooms, etc? Is there an attic, basement, or ample storage?

3. The systems—What type heating and cooling does it have? What type windows does the house have? Is the exterior brick, wood, or stucco?
4. The condition—Look beyond paint colors and old or ugly carpet! Are the hard floor surfaces in good shape? How do the cabinets and counter tops in the kitchen and bathrooms look? Is there anything that needs to be replaced? How old is the roof? Does the yard need a lot of work?

The listing agent should have a property condition disclosure that will tell if anything is defective or has had damage in the past. Do not rely solely on this documentation as it is only as valid as the honesty of the seller.

What is the process once I find a home I like?

Make an Offer Your Real Estate Agent will write the offer. The Purchase and Sale Agreement is a standard contract that is written with legal jargon and with blanks to fill in according to your specific situation. The following lists required information for the contract:
1. Purchase Price
2. Loan Specifics (type of loan, amount financed, if appraisal must meet or exceed purchase price, etc)
3. Closing Date (date papers are signed)
4. Ownership Date (move-in date which must be AFTER funds have been received by the seller) See Chapter 4: Closing Day.
5. Name as you want it to appear on the *Deed*
6. Closing Attorney (name, address, phone number)
7. Earnest Money Deposit amount —typically 1% of purchase price

8. Special Stipulations (contingencies like the sale of current home, seller concessions, etc)
9. Time the seller must respond by

Seller Counters/Accepts/Rejects Offer The offer will be submitted to the seller's agent who will present it to the seller or directly to the seller if there is no listing agency. The seller can either reject the offer (this is extremely rare), accept the offer, or make a counteroffer. The counteroffer can be a change in the purchase price, closing date, or special stipulation. These negotiations will continue until an agreement is made or until either party decides an agreement will not happen.

🔑**Once both parties have agreed on the terms of the contract, you have a binding agreement.**

4

Due-Diligence Phase

What are the steps after you have a binding agreement with the seller?

The contract specifies the time line for certain aspects of the due-diligence phase. This includes applying for a loan, giving the earnest money to the appropriate entity, completing inspections, and negotiating repairs. The first and most important step is to secure your loan. Detailed information will be covered in the next chapter.

Earnest money is given to and will be held by either the Real Estate Agency for the seller or the Title Company/Attorney for the seller. This is typically a check written by the buyer. The contract will specify who the Earnest Money will be made payable to. The buyer's agent can get the check where it needs to go. The amount will be credited to the buyer at closing.

Schedule Inspections–the contract will specify how many days the buyer has to make all desired inspections. This is most often less than 2 weeks. Your real estate agent will schedule these.

- **Home inspections** are not required, but highly recommended. Typically your agent will have recommendations of trusted inspectors. This will cost anywhere from $450-$1000 depending on your location and on the size of the house. During a home inspection, the inspector examines various aspects of the property, including:
- Structural Components: Foundation, walls, roof, and framing.
- Exterior Elements: Siding, doors, windows, and drainage.
- Roofing: Shingles, gutters, and chimneys.
- Plumbing Systems: Pipes, fixtures, water heaters, and sewage systems.
- Electrical Systems: Wiring, outlets, circuit breakers, and lighting.
- Heating, Ventilation, and Air Conditioning (HVAC): Furnaces, air conditioners, duct work, and thermostats.
- Interior Features: Walls, ceilings, floors, stairs, and railings.
- Insulation and Ventilation: Attic and crawl space ventilation, insulation levels.
- A **termite inspection** is also recommended. Most Mortgage companies will require this. It will cost between $100-$300.
- **Additional inspections** may be necessary if there is a swimming pool, apparent foundation damage, questionable function of the HVAC (Heating, Ventilation, Air Conditioning) units, etc. These require inspectors who are experts in the specific area.

After the inspections, the inspector provides a detailed report outlining any defects, safety concerns, and recommended repairs or maintenance. This report helps the buyer make an informed decision about the purchase, negotiate repairs or price adjustments with the seller, or, in some cases, decide to withdraw from the transaction if significant issues are discovered.

DUE-DILIGENCE PHASE

Negotiate Repairs by looking at the recommended repairs listed on the home inspection report. Your agent will help put together a Repair/Replacement Proposal to give to the seller. The seller will receive the list and can agree to the list or negotiate to come up with a list both sides (seller and buyer) agree upon. If an agreement cannot be made, the contract can be withdrawn and the earnest money will be returned to the buyer.

Schedule Appraisal This will most likely be scheduled by your loan officer or loan processor. You will be required to pay for the appraisal up front. The appraisal company will email a payment link to you. This typically costs between $600-$800.

- An appraisal is conducted by a licensed or certified appraiser. This process is typically required by lenders during the mortgage approval process to ensure that the loan amount requested by the borrower is justified by the property's value.
- During a home appraisal, the appraiser evaluates various factors to determine the home's value, including: number of bedrooms and bathrooms, is there a garage, size of lot, square footage, is there a pool, have there been upgrades to the kitchen and/or bathrooms, etc.
- The appraiser will conduct a thorough inspection of the property, take measurements, and photograph the interior and exterior. They will also research and analyze comparable properties and market data.
- After completing the evaluation, the appraiser provides a detailed report that includes their findings and the appraised value of the property. This report is used by the lender to determine whether the loan amount is appropriate and to assess the risk associated with the mortgage.

- A home appraisal helps protect both the lender and the buyer by ensuring that the property is worth the purchase price and that the loan amount is not greater than the property's market value.

🗝 **The contract is time sensitive. Make sure you are meeting all deadlines specified in the contract.**

5

Securing Financing Phase

This chapter is dedicated to all things related to obtaining your mortgage. Without your mortgage in place, you will not be able to purchase the home. Time is particularly of the essence when securing the financing for your purchase.

What is needed to finalize my financing?

Your loan officer will submit your application to the lender. A loan processor will be assigned to gather all pertinent information needed by the lender.

🔑It is extremely important to give the loan processor any requested information or documents as soon as possible. The loan process takes time and you will not be able to purchase the home without it.

Decide on the Downpayment Amount - A *down payment* is an initial, upfront payment made when purchasing a home. The loan processor needs to know this to determine the loan amount. It represents a percentage of the home's purchase price and is paid in cash at the time of closing.

Obtain Homeowner's Insurance (HOI)

- Get quotes from several agencies and companies.
- Consider using the agent/company who has your auto insurance since they can bundle your home and auto to save you money.
- Give the HOI quote and declaration page to your loan officer or have the insurance agent email it to the loan processor.

Lock Interest Rate - Locking an interest rate means securing a specific mortgage interest rate for a set period, typically ranging from 30 to 60 days, during the home buying or refinancing process. This protects you from interest rate fluctuations while you complete the necessary steps to close your mortgage loan. Here's a more detailed explanation:

How Rate Locks Work:

- **Agreement with the Lender:** When you lock an interest rate, you enter into an agreement with your lender that guarantees the rate you were offered will not change for a predetermined period.
- **Protection Against Rate Changes:** During the lock period, even if market interest rates increase, your rate remains the same. This can save you money if rates rise before your loan closes.
- **Length of the Lock Period:** Rate locks typically last between 30 to 60 days, but some lenders may offer shorter or longer periods. The length of the lock period can affect the cost; longer lock periods might have higher fees or slightly higher interest rates.
- **Lock Fees:** Some lenders may charge a fee for locking in a rate,

particularly for longer lock periods. This fee can be a flat amount or a percentage of the loan amount.
- **Extension Fees:** If your loan does not close within the lock period, you might need to pay a fee to extend the rate lock, or you may have to accept the current market rate, which could be higher.

How to Lock an Interest Rate

- **Discuss with Your Lender:** Talk to your lender about their rate lock policies, fees, and the length of lock periods they offer.
- **Choose the Lock Period:** Decide on an appropriate lock period based on your expected closing date.
- **Confirm in Writing:** Ensure the rate lock agreement is documented in writing, outlining the terms, lock period, and any associated fees.

Locking an interest rate is a strategic decision that can provide stability and predictability during the mortgage process, helping you manage your financial planning more effectively.

Provide Documentation – the loan officer will need to obtain several documents including but not limited to:
- Proof of Income - pay stubs, W2s
- 2 year work history
- 2 year housing history (rent or own)
- Proof of Assets - bank statements (if the statement says there are 4 pages, you must send all 4 pages), other account statements such as investment statements if requested
- Copy of Earnest Money Check

- Student Loan Statements if applicable
- Income Tax Returns for previous 2 years
- Letters of explanation for things required by the underwriters

By law, within 3 days of the loan processor receiving all necessary documentation, the application will be complete and you will receive an initial Loan Estimate (LE). This estimate is an overview of all aspects of the purchase. It includes the purchase price, down payment amount, the costs related to the loan, the title charges, and the government recording fees and transfer charges. It also gives the amount that's required from you in order to close on the loan. You will be required to sign this estimate. Your signature indicates only that you received the estimate, not that you to everything in the estimate.

What fees will be included on the Loan Estimate?

Common fees associated with the loan and the purchase of the home that will be indicated on the loan estimate include, but are not limited to:

- **Origination Fee**: A fee charged by the lender for processing the mortgage application. This fee typically covers administrative costs and is usually a percentage of the loan amount.
- **Application Fee**: A fee paid to the lender to cover the costs of processing the initial loan application and credit check.
- **Underwriting Fee**: A fee charged by the lender for the underwriting process, which involves evaluating the borrower's creditworthiness and the risk of the loan.
- **Appraisal Fee**: The cost of hiring a professional appraiser to determine the market value of the property. Most of the time this cost is paid prior to closing at the time of the inspection and will

SECURING FINANCING PHASE

be shown as a credit on the closing documents.
- **Credit Report Fee**: A fee for obtaining the borrower's credit report from one or more credit bureaus.
- **Title Insurance and Title Search Fees**: Title insurance protects the lender (and the buyer, if purchased) against potential legal issues with the property's title. The title search fee covers the cost of researching the property's history to ensure there are no outstanding claims or liens.
- **Survey Fee**: A fee for having a property survey conducted, which verifies the property's boundaries and ensures that the home is located within those boundaries.
- **Attorney or Closing Fees**: Fees paid to the attorney or closing agent who handles the closing process, including document preparation and coordination of the transaction.
- **Prepaid Interest**: Interest that accrues between the closing date and the first mortgage payment. This amount varies based on the closing date.
- **Property Taxes**: City and/or county property taxes will be included and will be prorated based on the date of closing and the date the taxes are due.
- **Homeowners Insurance**: Lenders typically require proof of homeowners insurance, and the first year's premium may need to be paid at closing.
- **Private Mortgage Insurance (PMI)**: If the down payment is less than 20% of the purchase price, the lender may require PMI, which protects the lender in case of default. PMI can be paid upfront or included in the monthly mortgage payment.
- **Recording Fees**: Fees paid to the local government for recording the mortgage and deed, making them part of the public record.
- **State and Local Taxes**
- **Pest Inspection Fee**: The cost of a pest inspection to ensure the

property is free from termites and other pests, which is often required by the lender. This is often paid prior to closing at the time of the inspection.
- **Flood Certification Fee**: A fee for determining whether the property is located in a flood zone, which can affect insurance requirements and costs.

Understanding these terms and the fees and their amounts is crucial for borrowers, as they contribute to the overall cost of obtaining a mortgage and can impact the affordability of the home purchase. Communicate with the loan processor any questions or concerns you might have.

What happens next?

After you have signed the LE and given the requested documentation to the loan officer or processor, the loan will go into the **Underwriting Process.**

Underwriting for mortgage loans is a specific process that focuses on examining and assessing both the borrower's ability to repay the loan and the value of the property being financed. The following are areas the underwriter will examine.

- Loan Application
- Credit Report
- Income Verification
- Debt-to-Income Ratio
- Asset Verification
- Property Appraisal
- *Title Search and Insurance*

SECURING FINANCING PHASE

- *Loan-to-Value Ratio (LTV)*
- Risk Assessment

Each of these steps involves thorough checks and verification to protect the lender from financial loss while providing a fair opportunity for the borrower to purchase a home. The process can take **a few days up to a few weeks.** The underwriter may require additional documentation, account statements, letters of explanation, etc.

🔑 **Always give the loan processor requested information as soon as possible. Sign all documents in a timely manner.**

6

Closing Phase

You are nearing the end! Closing refers to sitting down with the real estate attorney and signing the loan documents and other papers required for transferring the deed from the seller to you. The closing phase can be stressful if you have not been diligent along the way. There are several things that will be required of you during this phase.

What do I need to do the week before closing?

- **Schedule Closing** Your Real Estate Agent or your Loan Officer will schedule a closing time with your closing attorney or title company. It is best to close sometime around mid-day. This gives the lender time to get the loan package to the closing attorney. Signing before 2 allows time for the funds that need to be wired to be done before the wire cut-off time. Allow for at least an hour to have time to sign all documents and to ask questions.
- **Make arrangements for Moving** You do not officially own the home until after you and the seller have each signed the closing papers and the funds have been transferred to the appropriate

parties (lender, seller, etc). If this does not happen on the day of closing, you will not receive keys to the house and thus cannot take ownership the same day. It is safe to have movers come the day after closing.

- **Schedule Utility Services Connections** Contact the utility company at least 3-4 days prior to closing to start services at the new home and/or to have the utilities transferred from your current location. Depending on the utility company, this may be able to be done on their website. Some companies require proof of ownership such as a closing document before services can begin.
- **Final Walk-Thru** A day or 2 before closing your real estate agent will schedule a final walk-thru where you will make sure the house is in the same or better condition as it was when you signed the contract. Also make sure any repairs that were agreed on have been completed to your satisfaction.
- **Review the Closing Disclosure** You will receive a closing disclosure which is a detailed account of the costs for the loan and what other closing costs will be. This is similar to the loan estimate, but will have exact figures instead of estimated ones.
- **Wire the closing costs to the title company** Most attorneys require funds to be wired the day before closing since this guarantees the funds to be deposited in a timely manner. **ONLY WIRE FUNDS VIA THE SECURE ENCRYPTED SITE SENT TO YOU BY THE ATTORNEY OR TITLE COMPANY.** Wire fraud is real! If you have a question as to the validity of wire instructions, contact the closing attorney/title company.

What should I expect on the day of closing?

This is the day we have worked towards!

- Meet at the closing attorney's office. Please bring your driver's license—they will need to make a copy.
- Sign all the loan papers in the loan package and the papers required for recording the deed. The closing attorney has looked through all the papers that must be signed and is on the lookout for anything that does not look right. You can trust that what you are required to sign is correct. That's why you are paying for an attorney.
- After you have signed, the papers will be sent to the closing attorney for the seller who will be signing the papers for the sale of the property.
- Once received, the Title Company will wire the funds to the Mortgage Company and to the seller's attorney.

Once all the money has been swapped, CONGRATULATIONS! You are now the owner of the house!

What should I expect after Closing

You will be given the keys to the house after the money has been received by the seller's attorney and dispersed to the appropriate place. This usually happens the day of closing but might be the next day if the papers were signed later in the afternoon (after wire transfer cut off times) and the money is not received before the end of the day.

Over the next few weeks and months, you will receive many solicitations for purchasing mortgage insurance, paying for a copy of the deed, etc. These are scams! If you ever have a question whether something is legit or not, please don't hesitate to ask your real estate agent or closing attorney.

7

Conclusion and Re-Cap

It is the American dream to be homeowners! Hopefully this book has informed you what to expect when purchasing a home and will guide you in how to make home ownership a reality. Follow the keys found throughout this book for a stress free process. May your dreams of owning a home come true!

Main Keys

🗝 Before you begin seriously looking for a home, know what you can afford.

🗝 If your credit score is under 580 or your DTI is greater than 43%, consider paying off some of your debt and/or contacting a credit agency who can give you tips on how to raise your credit score.

🗝 Provide honest and accurate information on your application to avoid delays or denials.

🔑 Use a local lender or Mortgage Loan Originator who can respond quickly and give you top notch service.

🔑 The contract is time sensitive. Make sure you are meeting all deadlines specified in the contract.

🔑 Avoid making large purchases or opening new credit accounts during the pre-approval process until you close on the house.

🔑 Always give the loan processor requested information as soon as possible. Sign all documents in a timely manner.

🔑 Only wire funds via the secure encrypted site sent to you by the closing attorney or title company.

🔑 The home is not officially yours until all paperwork has swapped between the seller and the buyer and all money has been given to the appropriate entities.

8

Glossary

Closing - Closing refers to the final step in the real estate transaction process that includes reviewing and signing documents, paying closing costs, transferring title to the new owner, disbursing funds, and recording the deed. It is a critical phase that includes real estate agents, banks, title companies, and lawyers.

Credit Report - A credit report is a detailed summary of an individual's credit history, compiled by a credit bureau. There are 3 main credit bureaus–Transunion, Equifax, and Experian. The report includes personal information, such as name and address, as well as a record of credit accounts, including loans, credit cards, and lines of credit. The report lists the status of these accounts, such as the amount owed, payment history, and whether any accounts are in default or have been sent to collections. Additionally, the report includes records of public information, such as bankruptcies, liens, and judgments.

Credit Score - A credit score is a numerical representation of a person's creditworthiness, based on their credit history. It helps lenders assess the risk of lending money to an individual. The score typically ranges from 300 to 850, with higher scores indicating better creditworthiness.

Deed - A deed to a house is a legal document that conveys ownership of real estate from one party to another. It is one of the most important documents in property transactions, such as buying or selling a home. The deed includes specific information about the property and the parties involved, and it must meet certain legal requirements to be valid.

Debt-to-Income Ratio - The debt-to-income (DTI) ratio is a personal finance measure that compares an individual's total monthly debt payments to their monthly gross income. It's used by lenders to gauge a borrower's ability to manage monthly payments and repay debts. The DTI ratio is expressed as a percentage and is calculated by dividing total recurring monthly debt by gross monthly income. Most federal backed loans cap the DTI at 43%.

Down Payment - The down payment is the first payment made towards the purchase of a home, usually paid in cash. It's typically expressed as a percentage of the home's purchase price. For example, a 20% down payment on a $300,000 home would be $60,000. The remaining amount after the down payment is usually financed through a mortgage. The larger the down payment, the smaller the mortgage loan needed. A larger down payment can often lead to better mortgage terms, such as a lower interest rateThe down payment helps establish equity in the home right from the start, meaning you own a portion of the home outright..

Escrow - Escrow is a legal arrangement in which a third party holds funds, documents, or other assets on behalf of two parties involved in a transaction until certain conditions are met. In real estate transactions,

GLOSSARY

escrow ensures that both the buyer and the seller fulfill their contractual obligations before the deal is completed.

Equity - Equity in the context of real estate refers to the difference between the market value of a property and the outstanding balance of any liens or mortgages on that property. Essentially, it represents the portion of the property that the owner truly owns outright.

Interest Rate - An interest rate is the percentage of a loan amount charged by a lender to a borrower for the use of assets, usually expressed as an annual percentage of the principal. It represents the cost of borrowing money or the return on investment for lending money.

Loan-to-Value (LTV) - The LTV ratio is calculated by dividing the loan amount by the property's appraised value. A lower LTV ratio is favored as it suggests the borrower has more equity in the property, lowering the lender's risk.

Title Company - a title company is essential for ensuring the legality and security of real estate transactions, protecting both buyers and lenders from potential title issues, and facilitating a smooth and efficient closing process.

Title Search and Insurance - This process is conducted by the title company and involves checking the property's title records for any issues that could affect ownership, such as liens or disputes. Title insurance protects the lender and possibly the buyer from future legal claims against the property.

About the Author

My husband and I will celebrate our 30 year anniversary on June 25, 2024. We enjoy traveling, hiking, entertaining, and being with family and friends. Our favorite pastime is anything home related—new construction, rehabbing a home, building cabinets and other furniture. First time home buyers are my favorite to work with. I love helping them find a home and walking them through the entire process. We have 3 adult children and one grandchild on the way and are actively involved in our church.

You can connect with me on:
- https://www.901mortgage.com

www.ingramcontent.com/pod-product-compliance
Lightning Source LLC
Chambersburg PA
CBHW072056230526
45479CB00010B/1101